FAMOUS SCIENTISTS AND WHAT THEY DID

PRE-K SCIENCE SERIES

BABY PROFESSOR

EDUCATION KIDS

Speedy Publishing LLC
40 E. Main St. #1156
Newark, DE 19711
www.speedypublishing.com

A scientist is a person engaging in a systematic activity to acquire knowledge.

ISAAC NEWTON

was an English physicist and mathematician. He is widely recognised as one of the most influential scientists of all time. Newton discovered and formulated the laws of gravity and the three laws of motion.

LOUIS PASTEUR

was a French chemist and microbiologist. He was the one who discovered the process of pasteurization, a process that involves heating a food, usually liquid, to a certain temperature for a specific length of time, and then cooling it instantly.

GALILEO GALILEI

was an Italian astronomer, physicist, engineer, philosopher, and mathematician. Galileo developed telescopes and used them to make revolutionary observations about our solar system.

MARIE CURIE

was a Polish and naturalized-French physicist and chemist. Her achievements included a theory of radioactivity, techniques for isolating radioactive isotopes, and the discovery of two elements, polonium and radium.

THOMAS EDISON

was an American inventor
and businessman. He is
known for the invention
and commercialization
of the electric light bulb
and the phonograph.

CHARLES DARWIN

was an English naturalist and geologist. he formulated the theory of evolution. He established that all species of life have descended over time from common ancestors.

JAMES CLERK MAXWELL

was a Scottish scientist in the field of mathematical physics. James Maxwell brought together the ideas of electromagnetic fields.

ARISTOTLE

was a Greek philosopher.
His writings cover
many subjects including
physics, biology, zoology,
metaphysics, logic, ethics,
aesthetics, poetry, theater,
music, rhetoric, linguistics,
politics and government.

JOHN DALTON

was an English chemist,
physicist, and meteorologist.
John Dalton invented
the atomic theory.

JOSEPH PRIESTLEY

was an 18th-century English theologian, Dissenting clergyman and natural philosopher. He is usually credited with the discovery of oxygen.

NICOLAUS COPERNICUS

was a Renaissance
mathematician and
astronomer. He formulated
a model of the universe
that placed the Sun rather
than the Earth at the
center of the universe.

ALEXANDER GRAHAM BELL

was a Scottish-born scientist, inventor, engineer and innovator. He studied the human voice, experimented with sound and is credited with the invention of the first practical telephone.

ANDRE MARIE AMPERE

was a French physicist and mathematician. He was one of the founders of the science of classical electromagnetism.

BLAISE PASCAL

was a French mathematician, physicist, inventor, writer and Christian philosopher. Blaise Pascal along with Wilhelm Schickard was one of two inventors of the mechanical calculator.